The Tight Rope

Dialogues
Exploring
Balance
Wisdom
Mystery
and
Development

Ryan C. Taylor

Cover Art by Lindzor Parker

ISBN: 978-1-7324819-5-4

Check out Ryan's other books and projects at:
projectado.com

Contents

Introduction • 3

Part One – Chaos • 5

Part Two – A Musical Example • 9

Part Three – Play, Rest, and Work • 14

Part Four – Specialization and Generalization • 19

Part Five – Inductive and Deductive Reasoning • 22

Part Six – Practice and Application • 26

Part Seven – Relaxing Hard • 34

Part Eight – Exactness and Intensity • 41

Part Nine – The Developmental House • 43

Part Ten – Maps and Territories • 47

Part Eleven – Big Pictures • 50

Part Twelve – Exploring the Structure of Balance • 53

Part Thirteen – Exactly Half of What Exactly? • 58

Part Thirteen and a Half – Attractors and the Octave • 61

Part Fourteen – Integrity and Harmony • 63

Part Fifteen – Habits • 69

Part Sixteen – Completion and Mystery • 72

Conclusion – Inner Harmony, Peace, and Purpose • 75

Introduction

I tried to find a good quote to introduce this book with, but I failed to find one that was sufficiently inspiring. I was hoping to get something like the following:

True education is a confrontation with mystery. It is not mere memorization nor processing of information, though it may involve those things from time to time. The heart of education is to face the vast, chaotic, and unknown world, and to delve into its dangerous depths with humility and courage.

But anyway… I suppose many people might want or expect an introduction that describes what this book is all about. The trouble is that this book is about mystery, and so if I tell you any more than that it seems to defeat the purpose.

What's that? You want an introduction anyway? Well… okay. I'll give you a short one:

The following is a series of dialogues that came to me during a deep meditation. In their original form, these writings were both highly chaotic and very interesting to me. I have refined them over time while attempting to keep their original spirit intact. While the dialogues are a bit more orderly now, you should still be prepared for a heavy dose of chaos and mystery. As I've been starting to explain, those themes are a big part of what this book is about.

In addition, the following imaginary conversations explore the topic of how to create a balanced life. Rather than answering this question directly, these dialogues exemplify what the journey of exploring this question might look like. I believe that such an example is at least as valuable as any direct answers I could provide.

As a conclusion, I'll offer my reflections on how these ideas have influenced me and how they appear a couple months after their initial inspiration.

I invite you to get comfortable, relax, and enjoy the mysteries.

Part One
Chaos

There is a foe on the left and a foe on the right.

Therefore, you have to walk a very narrow path between them.

This is the tight rope of life.

I don't understand. Why are you talking about a tight rope?

We are faced with chaos. We need to organize things.

Why?

Because dealing with a small number of things takes fewer resources and dealing with a greater number of things takes more resources.

What is that supposed to mean?

To get organized is to think of things like they are arranged in a small number of categories.

This is useful.

What can you use it for?

Everything. Well… everything that's useful anyway.

Everything?

Everything that is useful needs to be organized.

Are you saying that all the important things have to be organized?

Useless things can be important too.

That doesn't make any sense.

If you understand the developmental hierarchy, it will make sense.

What's the developmental hierarchy?

We start with chaos. That's level one. Next, you learn that order is useful. That's level two. After that, you learn that chaos and order mixed together is better. Annnd after that, you learn how to get exactly the right mixture of chaos and order.

What's the right mixture?

Well, that depends.

Not helpful, Dad. How do I know how much chaos to use and how much order?

You have to make it so that exactly fifty percent of your problems come from chaos and exactly fifty percent of your problems come from order.

Exactly half?

Exactly half.

Why exactly half?

Well, let's see… If it's all chaos, you'll get nothing done. If it's all order, you'll never discover anything new. And then if you don't discover anything new, you won't make progress in the long-term.

In the long-term? What about the short-term?

For the short-term, you'll need the order. But for the long-term, you'll need the chaos.

Why?

Let's do it again. Order is useful for meeting short-term needs. Chaos will help you to discover new things. Then, once you have learned those things, you will get to the next level, but that will take time. So, that's why the path of chaos takes time. The path of chaos is long-term.

Ohh...

So where do you want to go from here?

Part Two
A Musical Example

Well, let's see. If I repeat back what you said, I can make sure that I understand. Why does repeating help you to learn things?

That's a great question. Well… I don't know. But we can try to find out. When I want to figure something out, I look into the chaos.

Wow, really?

Yeah. I look into the chaos, and I see what I find.

What are you finding?

Well, I suppose if something happens a lot it must be pretty important.

That's true.

Might be an evolutionary thing.

Ohh… interesting.

That's funny. Why are things funny?

That's the chaos part.

Ohh… And why do we have to balance chaos and order again? Like maybe it's fine to be really orderly or really chaotic. And actually… How do you know? Can you prove it?

Well, one way of proving something is to look at examples. Like the best pieces of art always have something novel and exciting and adventurous! But they are also grounded in something familiar, like the old structures that have always worked and that we have always relied upon.

Whoa… right.

If the piece of art gets too exciting, it stops working. Like a piece of music that just starts to sound weird. We call that kind of music avant-garde.

Avant-garde?

Yeah, I'll have to show you sometime. It's not that great.

I'll have to take your word for it…

But then, there is also another kind of music that's just the same thing over and over and it's been done a hundred times before. Like over and over in the same song. Or over and over in different songs. Or over and over in different years and centuries…

Yeah…

We call that kind pop music.

Really? Pop music? Is pop music bad too?

Well, pop is alright I guess but it gets pretty boring after a while. You never get to anything new. You never get to the next level, you know?

What's the next level?

The next level is where you try to get exactly the right mixture of chaos and order.

Okay, I think I understand what you mean, but I'm still not completely convinced. I think I might agree that some order plus some chaos is better than just one or the other. But I'm really not sure that it has to be exactly half and half. Like aren't there pieces of music that are a little more orderly and others that are more chaotic? And isn't that a good thing? We don't want all music to be the same, right in the middle, do we?

Surely, not. That would be terrible!

Then, how can you say that it should be exactly half and half?

Well, I never said that it should be half and half exactly… I said that exactly half your problems should come from chaos and exactly half from order. But if you look at it exactly, that's a little different.

I think I'm going to get frustrated with you pretty soon if you keep being all confusing and mysterious.

Mystery is an important part of life, as is patience.

Fine. How can you prove this whole exactness thing to me then?

Well as I said, one way of proving something is through examples. We call that ***inductive reasoning***.

Inductive reasoning?

Yeah, it might help to repeat it. That will help you to remember.

Okay… inductive reasoning.

Or maybe write it down too. That always helps.

Okay… I'll start taking notes then. Innnduuucctivvve reaaassoooonnning.

So, inductive reasoning is what I just did with the music that was crazy chaos or boring order. You got me?

Got it.

Okay, so then there's a different kind of reasoning. This one is called ***deductive reasoning***.

Okay. I wrote that one down too. Dad, can we play now? I'm bored.

Part Three
Play, Rest, and Work

Sure. Play is important. Go take a break and then we can come back to this.

Really? Play is allowed?

Play is actually super important. It's like fueling up your gas tank for the important adventures of life.

Okay, well now I'm playing, and I rested a while, but I'm still kind of bored.

When you are bored, that's a good sign that you are ready to start working on something.

What if I don't want to work on something? Playing might be boring but working on stuff is even worse sometimes.

That's true. Working can feel pretty bad sometimes.

Then, why go through all that?

If you sacrifice and work hard, you can accomplish great things.

Well, that's pretty cool, I guess. But what's the point of all that? Like… are spaceships and tall buildings really all that great? They are fun the first time, but after a while those are boring too! Everything is boring eventually. So, what's the point? I think I'm getting depressed.

I think you actually just stumbled upon something beautiful. Things **are** fun the first time. That's the chaos part. Chaos is a lot of fun. But an experience that is repeated eventually becomes boring. It's not new anymore after a while. That's when you know that you've gone too much in the direction of order.

Okay that makes sense. Yup, checks out. Okay, soooo… I'm still bored.

Which means?

I should move in the direction of order? And do something useful with my life?

Right!

But rest and play are still okay sometimes?

Also, correct!

Wait… Is this the tight rope thing again?

Correct for a third time in a row.

Ohhhh... We are back to where we started!

Okay, okay. So, let me see if I get this. When I've rested enough and had my fun, I might get bored eventually and that's when I should start working, right? But... what if there's a big problem? That's going to require work too, right?

Excellent, I'm going to call that win number four. So, you'll need to address all the important short-term problems first. Second, you can relax. And then third, you'll be ready to work on something new.

Ohh... okay. Wait... Is this like the developmental hierarchy thing?

It is, but we phrased it differently this time. Let's repeat it in another variation.

First, you start as a baby. That's total chaos. It's mostly pretty great fun, except when problems happen and then you are totally powerless. So, that kinda sucks.

Yeah.

So, let's call the baby step level one.

Okay.

Level one is total chaos, fun but powerless.

Level two is order. That's where you become powerful and do really amazing things.

Cool! Am I at level two? That's sounds pretty great.

You are at least a level two kiddo. Probably higher.

Nice.

Okay, so level three is where you learn that chaos and order need to be balanced.

Right. I think I got that one too.

Level four is where you learn that chaos and order need to be balanced exactly.

Yeah, this is the one that I keep getting stuck on.

Well… that makes sense. We need some new tools to really understand level four.

18

Like what?

Part Four
Specialization and Generalization

Have you ever heard that the whole is greater than the sum of its parts?

No… also that makes no sense. The sum of the parts should be exactly equal to the whole mathematically.

And yet… somehow in the real world they are not. For example, how much value does each part of a car have on its own? Each part of the car is primarily valuable because of its potential to create a whole: a functioning car. The human body is the same way. Each body part only produces value through its connection to the functioning whole.

I refer to this phenomenon as **emergence** because it is the pathway through which new wholes emerge into the world.

Emmeerrrggggeennccceee… Okay, I've got this one in my notes too now.

Each person is a valuable whole that comprises many parts. Each person can also be thought of as a part contributing to the larger whole of society. And each person takes on specialized functions in society. Through specialization, one person can become an expert in one thing while another becomes an expert in a different skill or subject. If a person specializes in one particular area, they will be able to go further in that domain than the generalist who expends energy in many areas. And if many specialists cooperate together, society can go far into many areas!

However, there is a problem. Sometimes, one can become too specialized.

How so?

A person who is too specialized will miss connections to neighboring subjects and to the bigger pictures of life. With fewer connections, there will be less synergy, less emergence, and ultimately less novel creativity.

Ohhh... wait, this is another tight rope, isn't it? That was fun the first time, but I think I'm getting bored of it now.

Have patience with it. The more tight ropes you see, the more you will really understand life.

Okay, but you said you would explain about how to get exactly the right proportions of chaos and order. How does all this specialization stuff help with that?

Well, to know how much chaos and order you need, first you will need to decide on your specialization.

Ohh... I get it. So, different specializations require different mixtures of chaos and order! That makes sense!

Right. And once you understand the specialized purpose of a particular project, creative work, or intention, then you can start making your recipe of chaos and order. Then, you can refine your recipe and try to get it more and more exactly right.

How do you do that?

Part Five
Inductive and Deductive Reasoning

Well, for that we will need some thinking tools.
Do you remember when I told you about
inductive and deductive reasoning?

Oh yes, I have notes about that. You never really
explained what deductive reasoning is though.

Let's review inductive first. Inductive is when
you learn from many examples. The many
examples show you a broader principle.

Got it.

Deductive is the opposite. That's when you start
with broader principles, reason things out using
logic, and finally arrive at specific conclusions.

Okay, kinda makes sense, but I think I'm gonna
need some examples. Or maybe some inductive
reasoning, I guess.

Right. So, an example of deductive reasoning
would be: Someone says that a rectangle is the
same as a triangle, and you are able to figure out
that they must be incorrect.

I don't get it.

What's the definition of a rectangle?

A two-dimensional object with four sides.

Right! And the definition of a triangle?

A two-dimensional object with three sides.

Yes. And therefore, can these two things be the same?

No.

No, they cannot. And how do we know?

Deductive reasoning?

Correct! Deductive reasoning! The kind of reasoning which makes use of abstract principles and logic.

Furthermore, once we understand that rectangles and triangles must be different shapes according to their definitions, then we can apply our knowledge to many specific situations. For example, we might ask if the foundation of a house is shaped into a rectangle or a triangle. And we can use the exact same reasoning to come to conclusions about the walls of the house or the sides of a pyramid or many other specific situations. In this way, deductive reasoning progresses from the general to the specific, whereas inductive reasoning progresses from the specific to the general.

Riiiight okay.

We start with little-picture stuff, developmentally speaking. Remember we started with a specific example of the tight rope idea, right?

Mmhmm. Chaotic and orderly music.

But now we are moving on to the big-picture stuff. That's where we understand the general conclusions that are supported by our little examples with inductive reasoning. After that, we can also apply our general conclusions to many situations with deductive reasoning.

Right. I got it!

So, now you are ready to start creating your own mixture of chaos and order.

Whoa, really?

For sure. To begin with, you can use inductive reasoning. That's where you look at your past attempts to achieve your goal and ask yourself if chaos created more problems for you or if order created more problems for you. Then, you move toward balance.

Like walking on a tight rope…

But remember, because of specialization, every situation will require a unique tight rope. So, you will have to evaluate your mixture of chaos and order continuously and adjust it all the time. I'll tell you, sometimes, it can be a whole lot of work.

That sounds like a real headache.

Well… only sometimes. Mostly, it is a whole lot of fun, because every time you get it exactly right, it feels amazing. It's like hitting the sweet spot.

Wow, I wanna do that! Wait… so what about the deductive reasoning then?

Part Six
Practice and Application

I will tell you about applying deductive reasoning to the tight rope one day, but I think for now you should practice with inductive reasoning.

Awww, but Daaaad. I'm ready for deductive reasoning. I know you are going to say be patient, but I already know about patience. I'm ready to move on.

It is not enough to know about patience. You must practice it. You must integrate it. Just as it is necessary to practice the tight rope and to practice inductive reasoning. Don't worry. I promise it'll be fun, and it will help you to see life more clearly.

Okay then... How do we practice?

The tight rope has many manifestations. The more you understand it, the more manifestations you will see. Let's examine a couple examples.

Consider the question of how to relate to evil. If we do not consider the real possibilities of evil, we will act naively and be taken advantage of. If we dwell upon the possibilities of evil for too long, we may become cynical and unwilling to cooperate with other humans. By defining these two errors, we can begin to describe our answer as a tight rope. We can adjust our perspective by first asking how much we suffer from being taken advantage of. Then, we can ask how much we suffer from aloneness, mistrust, and cynicism. Finally, we can ask which side of the tight rope causes more suffering. The answer to the last question shows us how to improve. If we have mostly been too cynical, we can challenge ourselves to open up and take social risks. If we have mostly been too naïve, we can challenge ourselves to question, scrutinize, and defend ourselves more fully. Through this process, we can find balance.

What is another question that we might be able to answer with a tight rope?

Does life matter or is it all just some kind of silly game?

Life is a balance between the serious and the playful. The seriousness of life honors the depth of people's pain, caring, and desire. Contact with suffering carries with it the most obvious kind of seriousness. All you have to do to see that is remove the faulty mental gymnastics which might make it appear otherwise.

The playfulness of life honors the vastness of space and time, and the opportunity to try again. If you fail today, perhaps you will succeed tomorrow. If you fail this decade, perhaps you will succeed in the next decade. If you die and your creativity passes away, perhaps another human will succeed where you have failed. If humanity is wiped out and its creativity passes away, perhaps another form of life will succeed where we have failed. There is always a way to try again. In the vastness of possibility, perhaps playfulness is the appropriate mindset.

But things are still partly serious, right? Just because we might have another chance, that doesn't mean that our current chance doesn't matter, right?

Quite true. The consequences are real, and they matter. Though, they do always pass into the expanse of history.

Is life meaningful or meaningless?

Life is full of meaning. Everywhere you look there are examples of meaning and intelligence and significance and patterned beauty.

Contemplate the miracle of being alive, the complexity of your own brain, the manifestations of the Fibonacci sequence in nature, or the beauty of music, and you will find meaning in abundance. Connect with another human and you will find the meaning of life, soul, and consciousness. Meaning is everywhere. To miss this is a form of blindness.

But you didn't answer that one with a tight rope. I thought you would answer with a balance between meaning and meaninglessness.

I'm glad we have run into a situation like this. Not all tight ropes are created equal and not all tight ropes are sensible ways of viewing the world. While we could in theory contemplate some form of balance between meaning and meaninglessness, these two polarities are not of equal value or importance.

It is true that many things are meaningless. However, to characterize life as a whole as meaningless is incorrect. Even those meaningless aspects of the world are part of larger meanings. Therefore, in this case, we should not balance the truth with a falsehood.

The real tight rope here is better expressed by your previous question. The balance is between playfulness and seriousness much more than it is between meaninglessness and meaning. Playfulness is a truer, more useful, and more positive version of the meaningless attitude.

Okay... well if there is meaning in the world, is it subjective or objective?

Now, that's a descent tight rope. Truth is subjective in that it is always perceived through a perspective and perspectives may even influence the reality of a situation. And yet, truth is objective in that our perspective will not override the reality of the world. If you walk into a wall, it will stop you in your tracks regardless of your opinion on the matter.

Okay, let's try a different topic. Society seems to be making a lot of mistakes. Should I even cooperate with society when they are like this?

Societies can build great things through cooperation. Even with messy and imperfect foundations, the many, integrated together, can specialize, unite their efforts, and go surprisingly far. However, the lone individual, while relatively powerless, is free to step outside of society and examine its mistakes. Without the anchor of consensus, the highly independent mind may drift away into madness or discover

the truths that everyone else has turned away
from.

*Then, the lone individual should listen to society
and society to the lone individual.*

There is balance between the individual and
society. There is another balance between
listening and expression.

Most people love to speak about themselves and
truly be seen. And yet, it is through listening
that we most directly expand ourselves. Moment
by moment, listening may not seem to expand
ourselves much. Perhaps, we hear only things
we have considered many times before. But if
you listen long enough and hard enough, you'll
catch a gem, and then maybe the first gem will
lead to a second, a third, and so on. Listening is
like fishing for gems. It takes patience.

But this is not to say that listening is more
important than expression, for when you have
something to say and when you feel the call
toward creativity, you have the opportunity and
perhaps even the responsibility of stepping forth
into the dangerous spotlight. Listening cannot
be an excuse for turning away from the truth
that demands to be spoken.

We must be both humble and brave.

How much risk should I take on?

How long can you wait for a big win? How many losses will such a win pay for?

How many details should I consider?

How much time can your big picture afford?

How much should I specialize into one area?

How much connectivity can your specialized efforts produce? How much depth can your generalizing connections produce? And what would you prefer: to specialize in specialization or to specialize in generalization?

How extreme should I be?

Moderately extreme or extremely moderate, depending on how you'd like to think about it.

How should I understand the feminine and the masculine?

As a tendency created through the vast passage of evolutionary time. The wisdom of nature and its evident messiness are to be found somewhere in there.

How practical is practical enough?

Practicality is more clearly understood as that which is short-term. The unpractical, the experimental, and the chaotically creative become practical given enough time. Be as practical as you need to be to relax in safety. Be as relaxed as time and space allow. Be as creative as you can be.

How else can I use the tight rope?

As you journey through your life, see if you can *feel* the tight rope. Notice the relaxation and notice the focused efforts. Do you feel balanced? Now? And now? And now?

Again and again, ask: what tight rope am I walking on now? What foe is on the right and what then might be on the left?

Can I get closer to the sweet spot? To that line which is exactly right?

Exactly… right… there.

Part Seven
Relaxing Hard

I've been trying to balance on the tight rope. And sometimes I feel like I'm getting really close, but it's never quite exactly right. I kept trying for a while, and I was trying to be patient, but I still couldn't get it. I'm getting a little frustrated to be honest.

Well, it will never be perfect. So, there is no sense in getting frustrated about that.

It will never be perfect? But I thought you said it would feel amazing when I get it exactly right!

Oh… yeah, I guess I did say that. But what I mean is that you can get it more and more exactly right. That's the game of life. To try to get it **more and more exactly right**. It can never be perfect because then the game of life would end, and there would be nothing left to do!

The idea is to make things more perfect but not perfectly perfect. Just more perfect is enough.

But if more perfect is enough, why are you so fixated on things being exact?

Hmmm… it's a little hard to explain with just words. Try this: How much can you relax? Can you relax really hard?

How can I relax hard? I'm going to get frustrated with you again. I mean I can't try at nothing. I can't focus on nothing.

Can you start by just relaxing a little?

Okay, I can probably do that.

And then maybe a little more?

Okay…

And a little more?

I'm starting to feel pretty relaxed now.

Remember when I said that relaxation is like fueling up your gas tank?

Yes.

Well, that's true but there's more to it. You can use relaxation to get super-fueled up, because, unlike a car, your gas tank can expand. You can put as much gas in there as you can possibly take and then… wheeeeew! You'll go *flying*!

Really? I wanna try! I wanna try!

We will try it in a minute but let me tell you something else first. The relaxation leads you into the chaos and that can be a little dangerous, but not if you prepare for it properly.

Whoa, okay. How do we prepare?

First, you have to address all your short-term needs. That's the level where you learn order. I think it's level two maybe. I can't remember.

Dad, you can't remember your own levels?

Well, the numbers we assign to the levels aren't that important. The important thing is what they mean. And the level we need right now is some amount of order to prepare for our adventure. Once you have that, you can relax really hard and then you'll go flying.

Okay, but I still don't understand how to relax hard.

Just relax more and more deeply. Don't focus on anything in particular. Focusing will make you tense up. So instead, open yourself up to everything all at once. Open yourself up to the vast, dazzling chaos. Are you there?

I'm there.

And you are feeling really relaxed, and you've made sure all your short-term, practical needs are taken care of, right?

Yeah, I'm good. Safe. And wow. It feels really nice actually.

When you are in that place, what's your impulse? What do you want to do?

I want to create things. I want to play!

Exactly! Play is the purpose of life.

But work is also. I think I really get it now.

Does it feel like it's working?

Yeah, it does. Wait, what are feelings? We haven't talked about that yet.

Feelings are a piece of the chaos thing.

Oh really?

Yeah totally. And thoughts are part of the order thing.

Whoa... so there are like associations between all these different ideas.

It's like a big web. Really big. Huge, like super vast, or... if you include all the potentials which have not yet even been realized, perhaps infinite. You could imagine it all across the sky as an interconnected web of ideas. And the end result is amazingly beautiful when you see it.

Whoa!! I mean I kind of see it.

Let me try to help you to see it better. So, there's all this complexity and it's dazzling and vibrant. That's what makes life so awesome! Well, at least partly. Because the dazzling complexity is chaos. It's hard to understand despite being beautiful. So, that's why we need order. Order helps us to function in the very complicated world that's hard to understand and which might even contain dangers.

The world is dangerous?

Sometimes, it is, yes. And it is important to defend against dangers. But don't worry about them *too* much because that will make you closed off and you'll never be able to relax. Relaxation will lead you to chaos, and it is important to delve into the chaos from time to time.

Wait so relaxation is associated with chaos? There are so many connections I can't keep them all straight.

That's okay. Be patient with yourself, and you will learn them eventually.

Okay. Patience is hard though sometimes when I get frustrated.

Patience can be very difficult to master, yes. It is also very important to master. Patience is one of the manifestations of the proper balance between chaos and order.

Really? Wait. Tell me more.

Patience means you have considered your long-term goals, but a person who is both patient and wise will also have considered their short-term goals.

Okay, but then patience isn't enough, is it? You also have to be wise. What's that all about?

Wisdom is to know balance: the proper balance between chaos and order, the proper balance between short-term and long-term, the proper balance between patience and aggression.

Wisdom is to know balance in all things.

Wow.

Wisdom is to fully understand the tight rope of life. The foe on the one side and the foe on the other and the necessity of walking the narrow path between them.

I think I'm really starting to get it! Okay, can we talk about getting exactly the right proportions of chaos and order again? That part has been really bugging me for a while now.

Part Eight
Exactness and Intensity

The exactness part is how you make it more intense. If you focus on the exact balance between chaos and order, that's when you can hit the sweet spot and the magic happens. That's the best part of a song you love or the light bulb moment that strikes you in a state of flow and immersion.

But in order for things to become more intense, you have to be ready for it. Which means…

Having your practical needs taken care of.

And achieving a state of deep relaxation which eliminates our unnecessary expenditures of energy. Only then will you be able to channel all your energy into exactly the right spot.

Riiiight okay. So, that's why we had to talk about relaxation before we talked about exactness and intensity.

Indeed.

In every situation, there are many tight ropes to balance upon. Every tight rope can be understood more and more deeply. Each can be understood inductively and deductively. Each can be considered intellectually and felt intuitively. The more of these various perspectives you can master, the more exactly you will be able to align your balance.

Wow, when I relax deeply and focus on the exact spot where I am in balance, I feel amazing!

That's great. You've learned how to access the magic of chaos.

I love chaos.

As wonderful as the chaos is, remember to be weary of it as well. Chaos can produce both wonderful advances and terrible mistakes. That's why you must test everything that you find in the chaos. And you'll have to repeat the tests to make sure you are getting things right. The more you repeat a test, and the more the principle you are testing holds true, the more you know you can rely on that principle. And once you get a really good one, you can make it part of your house.

My house?

Part Nine
The Developmental House

The house of your life. You start out with a foundation when you are young. Every piece of that foundation is a lesson you learned, something you came to believe is true. But sometimes people don't test those lessons very carefully, and certainly young children probably don't know how to test things. They simply don't think to test things. We have to learn about all that as we get older. So, people build their foundations as best they can, and sometimes later on they have some real, big problems in the basement if you understand my meaning.

With each level we rise through, we build another floor. And when there is a problem with one of the lower floors, it tends to cause problems on the upper floors too.

I really like that analogy. So, what does this house look like?

We start with little things. Little things like physical objects and physical needs. That's the basement. Needing to use the bathroom and needing to eat food and stay safe and warm. But then we realize that staying safe and warm and making sure there is enough food to eat... that all takes a lot of work. So, we start to learn how to work. And we try to work hard so that way we can stay safe and warm and well-fed for as long as possible. And we start to plan. How can we be certain that we will be safe and warm and well-fed for a long time to come? Especially, in a world full of dangers. That's the first floor.

Ohhh... that's order. This is the developmental hierarchy again!

That's right! For a while, we can rely on instincts and emotions to guide us, but eventually we will need a well thought out plan to rise to the next level. That's where we start to use inductive and deductive reasoning. We could call that the second floor.

As we mature, we start to tend toward the bigger pictures. Because we want to know what the point of all this really is. Staying safe and warm and being well-fed certainly feels good. But does that matter? Is there any significance to it? That's when we start to become philosophical and maybe even spiritual or religious.

So, is that what is on the highest floors of the house? Philosophy and spirituality?

And self-actualization and morality and contribution too.

And so… you are saying that these developmental levels aren't really stages that you just move on from. Instead, they are like structures that continue to exist and affect everything else in your life.

That's right! For example, even as you start to ponder philosophy, you still have to make sure your body is well cared for.

Right.

That is why the house metaphor is helpful for understanding development. It shows us that a problem in the basement can cause problems on all the rest of the floors which rest upon it.

If you are struggling with a short-term, foundational problem – say not enough to eat or being too cold – it's pretty hard to get anything done at the higher levels. You can't relax very well, and then you can't think very well. And you probably get pretty frustrated too and sometimes there are all kinds of problematic emotions floating around. And then… well, your house tends to collapse at that point. But that's okay. Sometimes, you just have to build a new house or fix the old one. However, you want to think about it.

And I imagine a leak on the top floor could cause problems on the lower floors too, right?

Absolutely, the whole house is interconnected. And sometimes that can make things difficult to understand. However, if we can identify which floors our various problems originate from, that will help us to maintain a well-functioning house.

So, what's at the very top of the house?

Part Ten
Maps and Territories

At the top, we begin to wonder about life itself. We wonder about everything all at once, the whole universe. What is the best category or set of categories to describe life in general? How should we think of the entire affair? Is it one thing? People call that oneness. Or is it two things? Some people have called that yin and yang or perhaps chaos and order. Is it three things or perhaps many more than that?

Why place life into a set of categories? I don't understand.

It is much like a map of the world. We draw maps of the world and create helpful descriptions of countries, towns, geological features, and so on. If it is a good map, it will accurately reflect aspects of reality, and therefore it will help us to navigate and to get to where we want to go.

However, any map will inevitably be forced into using simplifications. Some maps may capture lots of information while others may highlight only a few items, but all maps will describe only certain pieces of reality, and even that they will accomplish imperfectly. Despite their imperfections, maps are the only way that we can understand the world. Thus, we must use them and try to make them better and better.

More and more exact?

Now, you are getting it.

Okay, I see.

We could have any number of maps for the same piece of reality. Some of them will work better than others. For example, if we are trying to map out an island, we could divide the island into sections. And that would be sensible because that way you could walk to one part of the island and tell your friends to meet you in that section. But how many sections should you divide the island into? A small number of sections is easy to work with, but it isn't very accurate. For example, if you divided the island into just two sections, then your friend might have a hard time finding you on the right half of the island.

However, a high number of sections is harder to keep track of. For example, if we divide the island into one hundred sections, how will we quickly know where section 47 is? We'd have to put some work into something like that, but if we did put the work in, we could meet our friends at a very exact location. Once everyone arrives at section 47, they should have no trouble finding each other.

We could also imagine dividing the island into even more sections which might provide an unnecessary level of accuracy at a higher cost.

So, the enemy on one side is that a small number of categories is not very useful or powerful. And the enemy on the other side is that a large number of categories is expensive and takes a lot of work to manage.

So, what should we do?

We try to walk the tight rope exactly between the two enemies.

Exactly right.

Part Eleven
Big Pictures

I understand that we need to balance the complexity of our categories now. However, you said that as we grow toward the top of our house, we will want to consider the big picture of life. And that makes me want to consider the very biggest picture.

Could we describe the whole world with only one category? That would be the biggest picture of all, right?

Go ahead and try. You aren't going to like the results.

Okay. I think life is beautiful. Even with everything that's wrong, it is all part of something beautiful. So, that category can describe everything all at once.

It's a nice try but how can you really leave ugliness out of the equation? There is so much in the world that isn't right. There are so many mistakes and evil deeds. When you describe the whole thing as beautiful, while you might be quite correct in a certain regard, it also leaves out something very important. It leaves out a recognition of all that suffering.

Okay... well, maybe life is a balance then? Between chaos and order?

What about all the things that are unbalanced?

Maybe... Maybe, it's oneness! Oneness just means it's one thing. You can't go wrong with that.

Well, now you aren't really saying much about life at all. You are just addressing the emptiness, the one interconnected field that has no particular qualities that we can articulate.

As soon as we start to say anything at all, we move into multiplicity. That's why the ancient book the Dao De Jing says, "The Dao that can be expressed is not the eternal Dao." When we describe oneness with language, we place it into a limited box that does not capture the fullness of reality.

Even the term ***oneness*** runs into the problem that it leaves out all the ways in which life is about multiplicity. Of course, any map will leave something out. However, despite the limitations of language, we must attempt to describe life as best we can, because this is the only way to move forward. And it seems the best way to move forward is with some of these big-picture ideas like chaos and order. Does that make sense?

It's really starting to.

The trouble with a single category is that single categories always have an opposite which should be included into the description. So, small numbers of categories seem to address the big picture of life the best. Using many categories is complex and that complexity could be worthwhile, but to start with... Well, how about we start with chaos and order.

That seems pretty good.

And I'm not saying that we can't make it any better. Probably there are lots of ways to make it better, but that's a good start.

Part Twelve
Exploring the Structure of Balance

When are we going to learn about how to approach the tight rope with deductive reasoning? You promised we would do that.

What do you think we've been doing recently?

You mean we were already using deductive reasoning?

Sure! Learning about categories, maps, and the big pictures of life is all deductive reasoning.

And you never told me??

Well, we both had a lot on our mind at the time. But if you want, there is a bit more we could cover about how to apply the tight rope to your life with deductive reasoning.

Let's do it!

Well, in deductive reasoning we apply our understanding of the big picture. We can apply a big picture understanding of life's parts. In many ways, we've already covered that in our explorations of chaos and order. We could use other archetypes like yin and yang, the four elements, the nine personality types of the Enneagram, the eleven spheres on the Tree of Life in the Jewish Kabbalah tradition, and so on.

However, I think what is most needed at this stage is a big-picture *process* for balancing on the tight rope, a general process that is applicable to many specific circumstances.

Yes, that sounds valuable.

Here are my thoughts on the matter. First, when confronted with a problem, we must search for a relevant, valid, and balanced tight rope. For example, let's suppose you want to tell your friend about an amazing discovery, but the friend is busy, and this makes you frustrated.

You can ask yourself, "What problem would be similar to your problem and yet opposite to it in some important way?" We might imagine that if there was nothing important to say and no caring about the friendship that this would be an opposing kind of problem. Then, we might ask, "What has gone too far in one scenario and what has gone too far in other?" We then might conclude that a lack of caring has led to depression in one scenario while an excess of caring has led to obsession, pressure, and rigid attachments in the other. Now, we are poised to ask the final question: "What would it look like to suffer minimally from both problems?" We then might imagine a kind of passion that can easily adapt to people's desires.

But is such a passion really possible? It seems that as you step more into the direction of passion, rigid attachments will naturally follow.

It is a tricky business, but that doesn't mean that it is impossible. The key comes from understanding that the passion you feel for something and your desire to share it can be disconnected from the fixations that cause you to suffer when things don't go your way.

In this sense, it is possible to remain balanced on the tight rope while extending ourselves into two virtues at the same time. In this case, we extend ourselves into both passion and flexibility.

Whoa.

When mapping out a tight rope, remember to consider the specialized purpose of your efforts too. If the question is how to optimize a particular relationship or friendship, we must account for the style of that particular connection. Are these two people wanting lots of independence or lots of deep intensity? What are their personality types? Different specialized purposes will require different kinds of balancing acts.

Right, makes sense.

Some tasks may require the use of multiple tight ropes or other kinds of maps that can describe the situation in more detail. With many factors at play, we may also want to consider emergence. What will happen as these various options and balance points interact with each other?

That all sounds very complicated and hard to keep track of.

That's true, and it is not always necessary to think through every detail consciously. That's why you have a subconscious.

A subconscious? What's that?

The subconscious handles an enormous number of little tasks: everything from the beating of your heart to the detailed processing of concepts into medium and big pictures that the conscious mind can work with.

Whoa... Can you describe the subconscious? Or give me a map of it?

You can think of it as a large number of subpersonalities that are connected together into one autonomous person, with a conscious mind at the helm. You'll learn more about all that very soon.

Part Thirteen
Exactly Half of What Exactly?

You introduced the tight rope as a situation where there is a foe on one side and a different foe on the other. But based on our last thought experiment, it looks like you could also think about the tight rope as being a friend on one side and a different friend on the other side. The tight rope doesn't always have to focus on negative problems, does it?

It is good to think about the positive side of the equation as well. However, the problems on each side of the tight rope show you what it looks like to go too far in one direction or another. And when you see the problems on both sides you gain a very specific map for optimizing your path forward. With the positive benefits on each side, there is not really a way to see what too much looks like on one side or the other, and therefore you may struggle to see the exact path you need to walk.

Though perhaps there is more for us to uncover in terms of working with the benefits on each side of these polarities. I'm not quite sure.

Interesting.

For one thing, I would definitely consider both the benefits and the possible drawbacks of a particular specialization before committing to it.

Makes sense. And when we pick a specialization, that won't necessarily be balanced right? That's why we don't necessarily want half chaos and half order for every situation. But I remember you saying that one should strive to have half their problems come from each polarity. Can you explain that again? Or maybe just explain it better?

You are correct in that every tight rope has a particular specialization, which involves different proportions of chaos and order. Once the specialization has been established, we can ask ourselves, "What is too much chaos or too much order for this particular situation?" In this sense, one step to the left is one degree of badness moving too much into chaos and one step to the right is one degree of badness moving too much into order. And therefore, by our own definitions, the person at the middle point faces problems that are exactly half on account of things being too chaotic and exactly half on account of things being too orderly.

This mental model is how we utilize exactness to produce intensity. This is how we can achieve intensely good results. This is how we can hit the sweet spot.

I see! But... it won't ever be perfect. You'll never be that imaginary person exactly in the middle. So, this mental model is, in a way, giving ourselves an impossible goal.

The perfect version of any goal is impossible. The idea is to try to get as close to your goal as you can.

I see. I see.

Just like balancing on a tight rope, everything is constantly in motion. One effort toward balance leads you too far in one direction and another effort leads you too far in the other direction. In the chaotic seas, you will never be stationary in your balancing act. You will never eternally and perfectly rest over the external and perfect balance point.

But you can taste the imperfect exactness that comes from getting oh so close...

Whoa... And... Is that really enough?

It's more than enough. It is the beautiful and endless game of life.

Part Thirteen and a Half
Attractors and the Octave

You've said that you can never achieve perfection, and I believe I agree. However, I had this one experience where it felt like I hit the sweet spot of the tight rope really, really well. I wouldn't describe it as perfect, but I would say that I hit something definitive. It felt like I crossed a threshold for a period of time. The threshold was an abrupt transition, and on the other side of it, things really started working in a new way. There was a feeling of creative emergence.

I've decided to name these kinds of thresholds "attractors" because there is an attraction or motivation to reaching the other side of some important line or edge. What do you think of my new creation??

I think that's a great name for that kind of phenomenon. This is a wonderful insight!
I'm realizing now that I may not have been clear enough before. Though we cannot achieve perfection, we can achieve our goals in a very satisfying and real way.

Right, I think that's what I have been realizing.

We could use another musical analogy for this concept. In music, an octave is a pair of two notes where the higher note produces a frequency double that of the lower note. In other words, the two notes are related by a 1:2 ratio. The octave sounds stable and harmonious. What's interesting is that if a pair of notes is slightly smaller or larger than an octave the ratio between the notes will become very complex and the sound of the notes will become discordant and full of tension. In such situations, the listener will often feel a pull or an attraction for the notes to shift into an exact octave where the music will feel stable and harmonious. The closer you get to the octave without landing on it exactly, the higher the tension gets.

Yes! That's exactly like my experience!

Sounds like you are making great progress. I look forward to seeing where your journey takes you next.

Part Fourteen
Integrity and Harmony

I've been applying the tight rope in as many situations as I can, but I often forget about the things I've learned. I don't see how to apply the tight rope to a situation while I'm in it. It's only days, months, or even years later when I look back that I realize how I was out of balance and what the balance was that I needed to align with. There are other times when I've already figured out the correct answers intellectually, but for some reason I just don't end up enacting what I know to be right! It's very frustrating.

Either it seems I don't have enough self-discipline or sometimes I don't remember what I learned. It's only later that it all comes back to me. Other times, I learn something, and I remember it too. But over time it feels less and less important, and I forget about the details that surround the lesson also. Then, something will happen, and I will realize how much I've really forgotten!

My question is: How can I use the tight rope fully? How can I go beyond mere intellectual understanding? How can I integrate the wisdom that I encounter deeply into my being?

Such a deep question really reveals your extraordinary development kiddo. I'd say the student is about ready to surpass the master. There are but only a few essential things left for me to teach you. Then, it will be your job to go beyond my level, and to find out what's next in the great adventure of life.

Dad, you're getting distracted. How can we learn the tight rope to the fullest extent possible?

I think the next level is integrity and harmony. You can imagine yourself as a collection of subpersonalities working together, like I mentioned before. There is your inner child, your inner adult, your inner artist, your inner scientist, your inner romantic, your inner jester, your inner warrior, and so on. If these subpersonalities are in conflict with each other, the whole person will be weak, and they will suffer through the confusion of their chaotic inner world. If the subpersonalities are in harmony with each other, the whole person will be strong and will take advantage of their inner harmony and cooperation to direct all of their being toward productive and creative intentions.

Oh, I see! So, that's like you and me, isn't it?

What do you mean by that?

I'm the inner child and you're the inner parent.

Please, let's refrain from breaking the fourth wall. It's distracting.

Okay, okay, so how can understanding subpersonalities help me with my question?

When a person's subpersonalities are in alignment, the person is in integrity. For example, if a person believes in health and fitness and regularly talks about the importance of diet and exercise, but then they do not treat their own body well, they have fallen out of integrity. This person has become a hypocrite. But if the person's actions align with their words, beliefs, and conscious intentions, then they will achieve integrity.

When a person understands the tight rope only to a shallow level, they will align some parts of themselves with balance but not others. When a person understands the tight rope deeply, they will align many parts of themselves together in a powerful integration.

I see! I see! So, I am only able to use the tight rope inconsistently, because not all of me is in integrity with my conscious beliefs and intentions!

That's right and now that we understand the problem, we can work on the solution.

Okay, what's the solution?

To learn something deeply, we must make use of three principles: repetition, variation, and association. We can see these principles operating in the best pieces of music, which make use of a few central themes, many variations, and many, many connections between all the elements of the music.

Repetition emphasizes importance. In combination with variation, it becomes much more powerful. Repetition with variation allows us to examine the principle of the tight rope – or any principle for that matter – in its many manifestations. As we learn more and more manifestations of the tight rope, we learn the concept more deeply. Each manifestation is a variation and yet also a repetition of the core concept. And among all the variations lies a vast network of associations that we may understand ever more completely.

Every variation allows us to address a particular subpersonality which may be out of balance.

I was following you up until the very last part there.

Well, let's examine our previous example about the person interested in being fit and healthy. Perhaps, they understand the tight rope a bit, though they haven't explored the concept very thoroughly. Generally speaking, they might understand that balance is important, and they might even understand that one form of balance is the relationship between rest and striving for growth. But perhaps they never quite considered that these principles apply to their physical fitness. Perhaps, they forgot that in this area too, rest is very necessary! Or perhaps, they engrained a habit of resting too much. In this example, the person understands the principle but must also consider a specific application to succeed.

Or perhaps there is some reason or some event in their past which makes it particularly difficult or emotionally painful to apply the principle of balance in this specific context.

Quite right. And so, if we suppose this person has a habit of resting too much, we could also say that their inner child is dominating their inner parent. Whereas, if they have a habit of working too hard, we could say that their inner parent is dominating their inner child.

I see! So, every form of tight rope can be thought of in terms of a metaphor between two types of people, like a parent and a child. Or an artist and a scientist. Or the person interested in fitting in and the person interested in standing out.

Just so. These characters that you refer to are archetypes – the patterns of emotion, thought, and action that repeat in variations throughout time.

Part Fifteen
Habits

You mentioned that the hypothetical person we discussed earlier might have developed a habit of resting too much. That makes me wonder if habits are important to understand for this topic. Now that I'm thinking about it, I often feel that it is because I'm operating with bad habits that I forget to apply what I know about the tight rope.

A wonderful insight! Habits are formed through repetition. Habits are useful because they allow us to perform actions without expending too much energy on them. They become part of our subconscious and run efficiently in the background. That's the good news. The bad news is that we must use lots of repetition to change our habits and that takes lots of time and energy.

We can think of conscious habit management as a multi-step process:

First, we must know with adequate certainty which habits we want to form and which we want to discard. Such certainty is acquired through intuition, inductive reasoning, and deductive reasoning. Keep in mind that it is impossible to be absolutely and perfectly certain of anything at all. So, shooting for adequate certainty is the correct target.

Second, we must bring ourselves into integrity with our goals and intentions. We propose or even declare to the kingdom of the self that a new intention has been created! We then open up the floor for objections, complaints, and questions from the many subpersonalities. We may choose to modify our intentions based on these inner conversations or we may choose to proceed forward as originally planned. When all the inner voices have been adequately listened to, we shall solidify our intention and then commit to it with the necessary strength that it requires. At this stage, the conscious mind must lead the kingdom of the self with purpose and clarity.

Third, with a foundation under our feet of adequate certainty, quality, and breadth, we may begin to build our habit with repetition. Here we make use of the three principles of deep learning: repetition, variation, and association. Over time, the intention will be manifest in every part of our being and then in every part of our lives.

As I have been learning with you, I have been developing habits, but I didn't really consciously choose which habits to develop. It is just that we ran into certain situations again and again in different forms.

You can also use the principles of repetition, variation, and association while you are discovering something new. And that's what we have been doing all along. Sometimes, you may not fully understand where you are going until you get there.

However, now that you understand the learning process, you can apply your understanding to your conscious goals and desires.

So, we can apply these same principles of learning both to our conscious goals and to our the more mysterious explorations of the unknown.

You've got it. So… where do you want to go from here?

Part Sixteen
Completion and Mystery

*The house, inductive and deductive reasoning,
specialization, balance, the tight rope,
learning... it is all connected! It's like I can
almost see the full picture of how it all fits
together, but it is not quite clear in my mind.*

Through repetition, variation, and association, it
will become more and more clear.

*Can you help me to see the big picture? Can you
describe how all these pieces fit together?*

The tight rope teaches us about the beauty and
usefulness of balance – exact balance, imperfect
balance, dynamic balance, and specialized
balance. But to really understand these things,
you must work with the house of development.
You must understand how balance is created or
disturbed at every level of your house. You must
see the balance in the small details and in the
big pictures. To work with your unique,
specialized house and to move around between
the different floors, you need tools like
inductive and deductive reasoning, intuition,
habits, repetitions, variations, and associations.

I see. That helps.

If you can see that, I think you are ready to graduate from my teachings.

Before I graduate, I want to integrate the tight rope into myself as a deep habit which harmonizes with all of my subpersonalities. How many variations do you think I will need to conquer before I really understand the tight rope deeply?

There is no such number of variations really. And this – I believe – is the last thing that I must teach you. If you know the formula for creating balance and depth, then you may apply it whenever and however you see fit! The tight rope can serve you now as a new tool, a new lens, a new floor of your house. You are ready to become your own teacher. You are ready to begin new adventures.

I hope that you will think of these conversations often in your travels, because the game of the tight rope is amazing! It is fun and fulfilling, intense in its exactness and forgiving in its moderations. It is joyful and endless and beautiful. It is my gift to you if you choose to accept it.

There is no need to master every variation right now or even eventually. You need only the formula. And you have that now, don't you?

I do! Or... I think I do. But it still seems a bit mysterious.

That's good! Mystery is one of the most beautiful things about life.

Are you sure that we shouldn't repeat it all one more time?

Oh, we should.

We should repeat it again and again.

We should repeat it in variations.

We should repeat it dynamically.

Experimentally.

Creatively.

Imperfectly.

Nearly continuously, and almost infinitely.

~The End

Conclusion
Inner Harmony, Peace, and Purpose

The weeks and months following my initial writing of this book were sometimes joyful and sometimes painful. Focusing on the tight rope idea clarified my desires, but at times it also seemed to increase my suffering when my life failed to turn out the way I wanted it to. Through these experiences, I realized that while writing about the tight rope idea I had, in fact, been falling off tight ropes left and right. Such is the imperfect nature of life. I had to revisit my understanding of Buddhist "non-attachment" more than once.

That said, from my current vantage point, I am still quite inspired by the tight rope idea, and I feel I've now achieved a greater level of balance because of it. I have worked to balance my desire with my relaxation, my focus on others and my focus on myself. I had to disturb and then reintegrate my inner harmony, peace, and purpose. Many forms of balance have come into clarity, producing many forms of value along the way.

For me, the tight rope has been a particularly useful perspective for creating music and art, as well as for enhancing my communication, writing, and relationships. However, it seems as though the potential applications are all around us in great number.

I am left wondering about the ways in which this book is still less than complete, less than balanced. Of course, there is much that has not been included here.

However, I feel (and hope) that at this point that this sense of incompleteness is more inspiring than problematic. This book seems by its nature to be provocative. It seems to point to possibilities within the reader for future adventures. It does not claim to be a comprehensive account of anything. That wasn't the point.

Setting aside questions of correctness and completeness for a moment, I wonder what this book has provoked within you. I wonder where you felt the most intense reactions and what those reactions might mean for your personal journey through life. Regardless of any potential disagreements or confusions, what did this book inspire within you? Perhaps, there is something to learn here that comes not just from the book itself, but from your own thoughts and intuitions which arise as responses to the experiments and provocations of these dialogues.

Afterall true education is not something I can give without your enthusiastic participation. Rather, it arises out of a declaration that your mind, body, and spirit are your own.

True education is a confrontation with mystery. It is not mere memorization nor processing of information, though it may involve those things from time to time. The heart of education is to face the vast, chaotic, and unknown world, and to delve into its dangerous depths with humility and courage.

Check out Ryan's other books and projects at:

projectado.com

Other books written by Ryan Taylor include:

THE MANTRA OF ADOGA
Profound Practices for Personal Growth

ADOGA
A Science and Spirituality of Profound Patterns

THE THEORY AND CREATION OF MUSIC
A Comprehensive Guide to Composing Your
Own Music